Favorite Hymns and Gospel Songs for Accordion

by David DiGiuseppe

Complete with fingering, left-hand notation and chord symbols

Easy arrangements

© 2017 by Mel Bay Publications, Inc. All Rights Reserved.

WWW.MELBAY.COM

Mel Bay Presents
Accordion Books by David DiGiuseppe

The Mighty Accordion
The Complete Guide to Mastering Left Hand Bass/Chord Patterns

A truly unique and much-needed guide to learning and mastering bass/chord patterns. For the beginner, the first few chapters assume little or no knowledge of the instrument and teach how to play simple accompaniment patterns. For the intermediate player, numerous exercises using the major, minor, seventh and diminished chords are included to develop skill in executing various bass/chord accompaniment patterns. For the advanced player, latter chapters present exercises on chord combinations needed to play sixth, minor seventh, major seventh, ninth and other advanced chords. Play along with audio featuring many of the book's exercises played at both a slow and moderate tempo.

100 Irish Tunes for Piano Accordion

From *Apples in Winter* to *The Wise Maid*, this collection of Irish jigs, reels and polkas provides beginning to advanced players with a wealth of traditional Irish music for solo keyboard accordion. This collection includes a number of tunes transcribed from recordings of not only the keyboard accordion, but also the Irish button box and concertina. With fingerings, ornamentation, left hand notation and chord symbols included, this book will allow even the novice accordionist to join in a traditional Irish session. Audio files feature 21 of the book's 100 selections.

100 Tunes for Piano Accordion

An extensive collection of reels, jigs, hornpipes and polkas from the French Canadian, Cape Breton, Scottish, Shetland, New England and southern old time traditions arranged for the piano accordion. Written with the beginner as well as the advanced player in mind, the arrangements are complete with ornamentation, fingerings, left hand notation and chord symbols. Appropriate for any G clef instrument.

Learn Blues Accordion
A Comprehensive Guide to Mastering the Blues

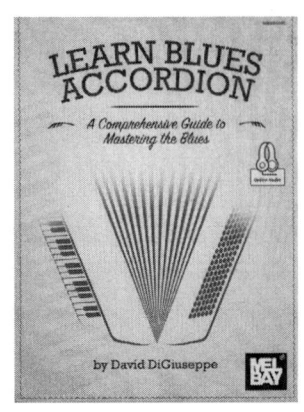

A unique method book that includes 34 blues compositions and numerous exercises. The material starts easy and progresses in difficulty as new concepts and techniques are introduced. The book explores blues scales, chord progressions and common blues techniques such as grace notes, slides, pedal points, double stops and tremolos. Left hand accompanying rhythmic styles are taught including boogie-woogie, the blues, shuffle, New Orleans and walking bass lines. This book also features exercises on comping chords in common blues keys using various rhythmic patterns. Includes accompanying audio.

Contents

Abide With Me 4
Amazing Grace 5
At the Cross 6
Blessed Assurance 7
The Church in the Wildwood 8
Count Your Blessings 9
Does Jesus Care? 10
Fairest Lord Jesus 11
Further Along 12
Give Me That Old Time Religion 13
He's Got the Whole World in His Hands 14
Hold to God's Unchanging Hand 15
I Feel Like Traveling On 16
In the Garden 17
I Shall Not Be Moved 18
It Is Well With My Soul 20
Just a Closer Walk With Thee 21
Joshua Fit the Battle of Jericho 22
Just Over in the Glory Land 24
Leaning on the Everlasting Arms 25
Love Lifted Me 26
Near the Cross 28
Nearer, My God, to Thee 29
O Come, Angel Band 30
The Old Rugged Cross 31
Onward, Christian Soldiers 32
Precious Memories 34
Rock of Ages 35
Shall We Gather at the River? 36
Softly and Tenderly 37
Swing Low, Sweet Chariot 38
There is a Fountain 39
The Unclouded Day 40
We'll Understand it Better By and By 41
What a Friend We Have in Jesus 42
When the Roll is Called Up Yonder 44
When We All Get to Heaven 45
When the Saints Go Marching In 46
Will the Circle Be Unbroken 48

Right Hand Fingering

Right-hand fingering is suggested for all songs. A number placed over a note indicates which finger to use (thumb is #1, little finger is #5). This sets the hand in a certain position. For example, if a 1 appears over a C note, it is implied that the second finger sits over D, third finger over E, etc. The hand stays in this position until fingering notation indicates a new position. Fingerings are not indicated for repeated passages: in these instances, use the same fingering as previously shown.

Abide With Me

Music by William H. Monk

Amazing Grace

Traditional

At the Cross

Music by Ralph E. Hudson

Blessed Assurance

Music by Phoebe Palmer Knapp

The Church in the Wildwood

Music by William Savage Pitts

Count Your Blessings

Music by Edwin Othello Excell

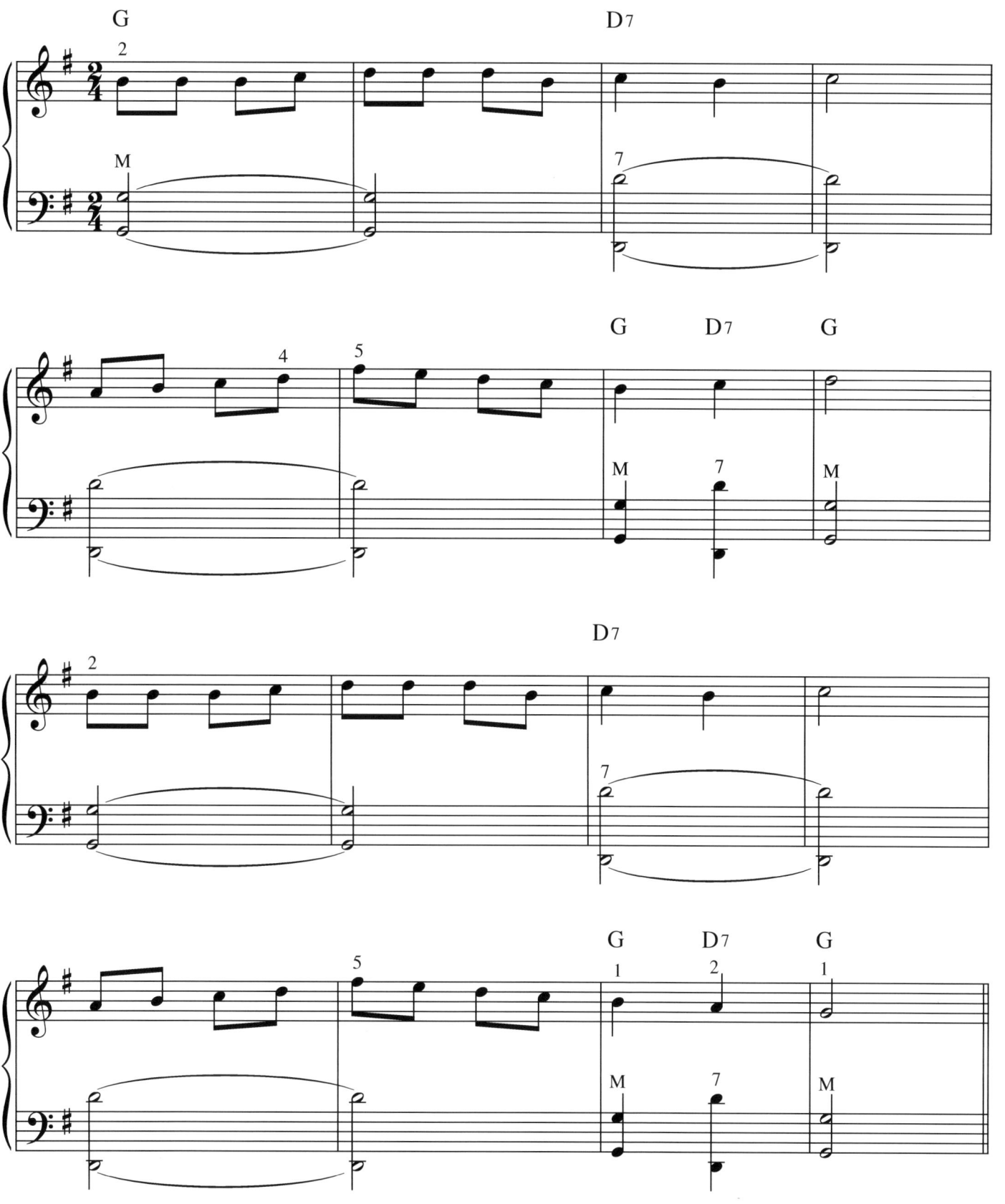

Does Jesus Care?

Music by J. Lincoln Hall

Fairest Lord Jesus

Further Along

Music by W. B. Stevens

Give Me That Old Time Religion

African American Spiritual

He's Got the Whole World in His Hands

Traditional

Hold to God's Unchanging Hand

Music by Franklin Lycurgus Eiland

I Feel Like Traveling On

Music by William Hunter

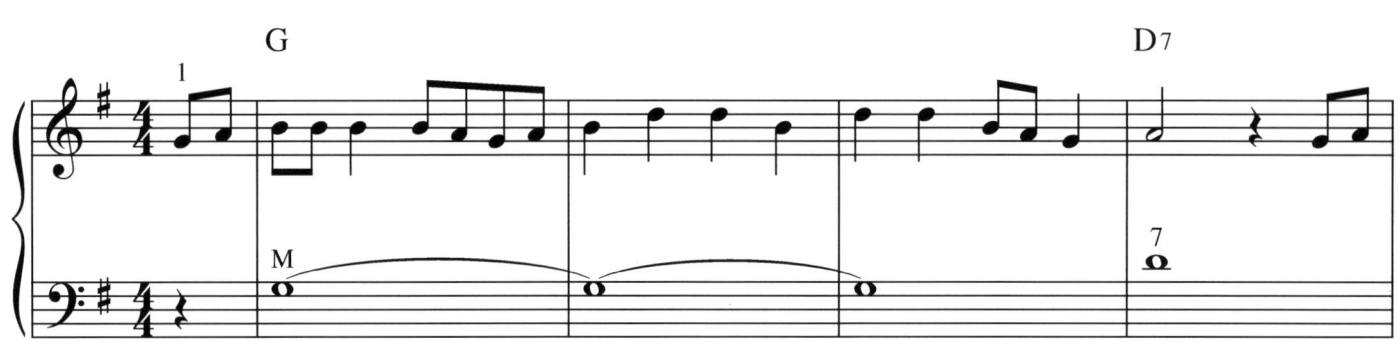
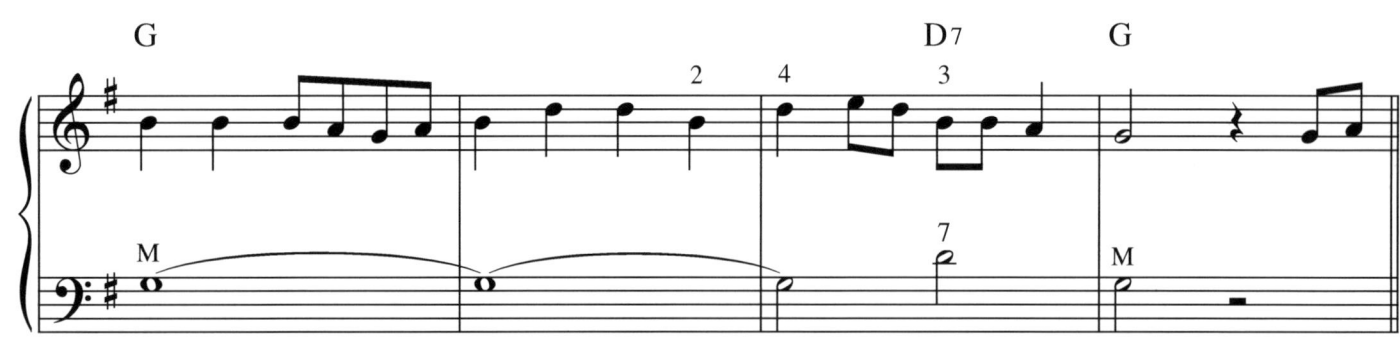

In the Garden

Music by C. Austin Miles

I Shall Not Be Moved

African American Spiritual

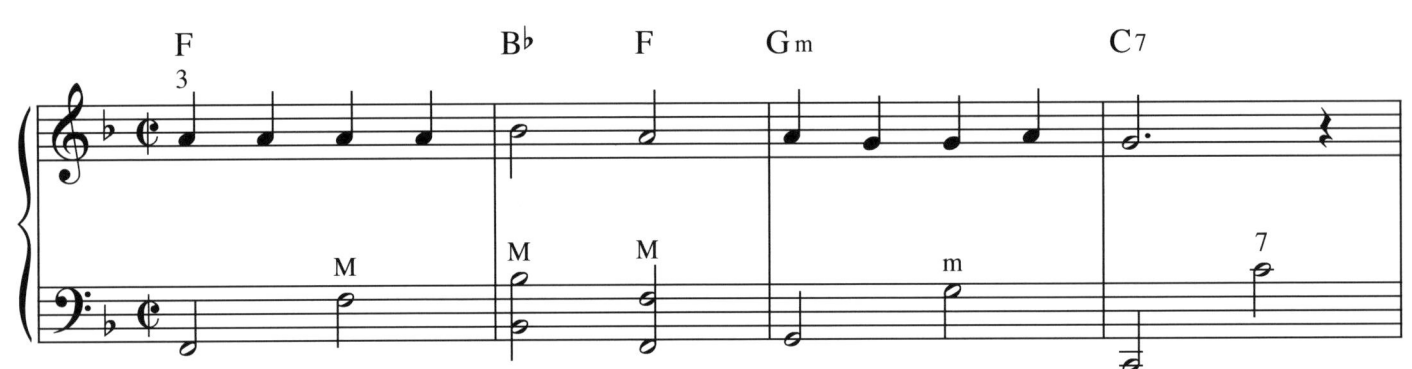

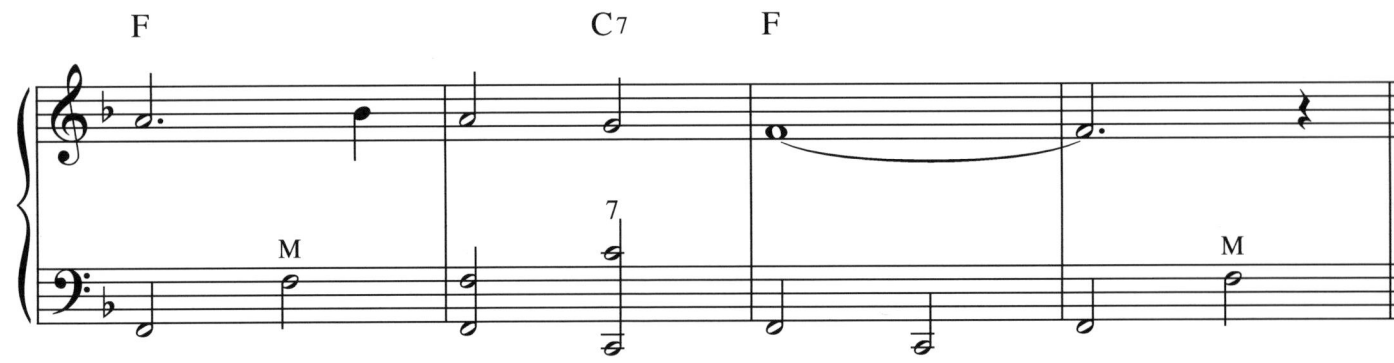

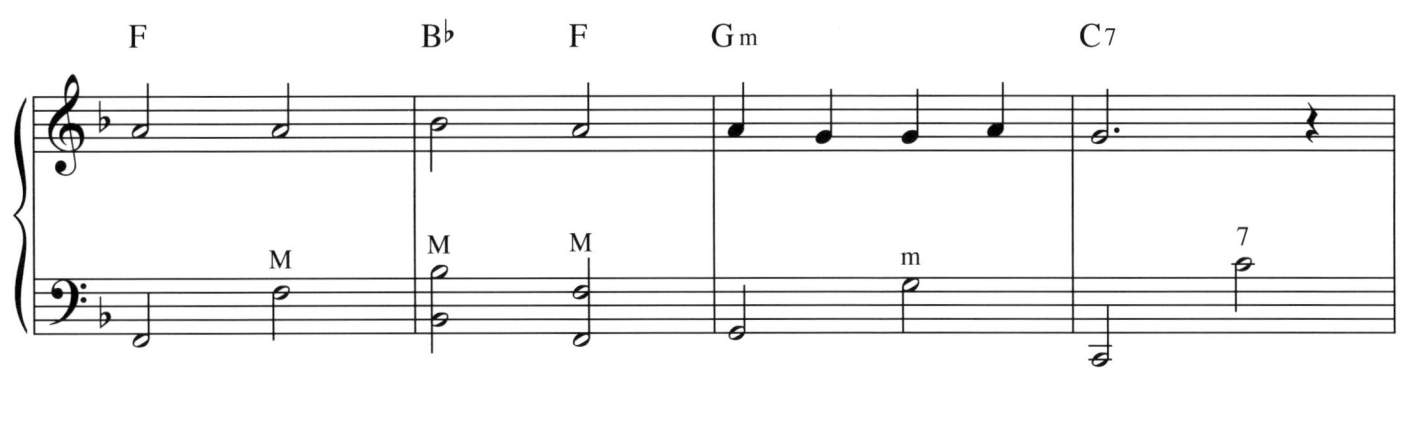
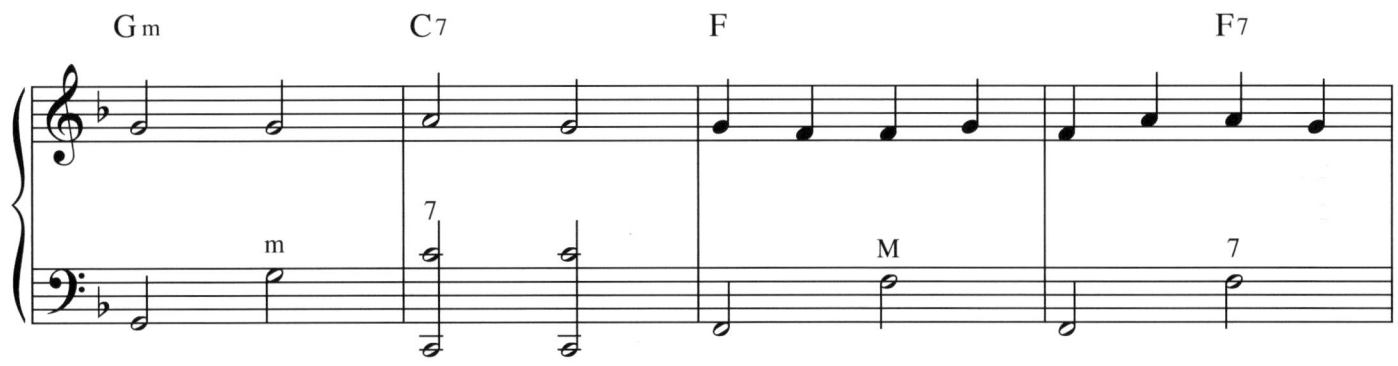

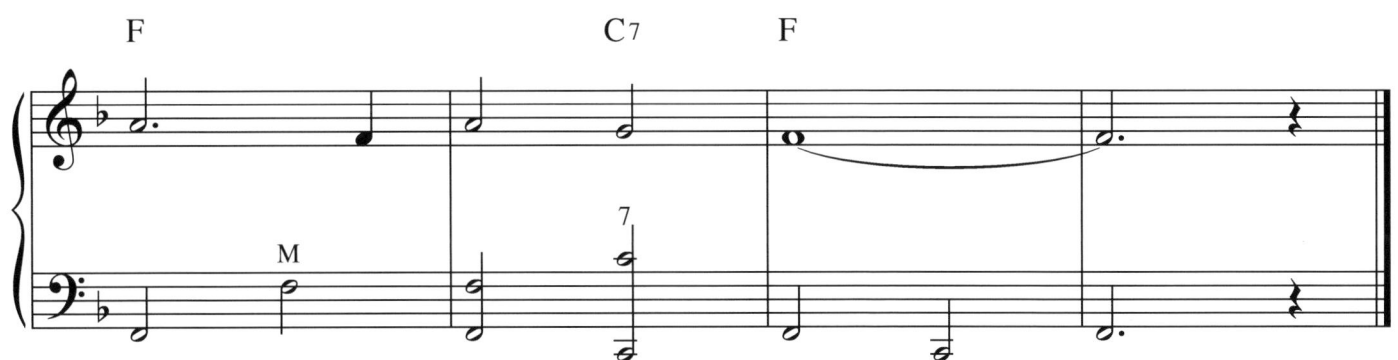

It Is Well With My Soul

Music by Philip P. Bliss

Just a Closer Walk With Thee

Traditional

Joshua Fit the Battle of Jericho

African American Spiritual

Alternate 2nd part

Just Over in the Glory Land

Music by Emmet Sidney Dean

Leaning on the Everlasting Arms

Music by Anthony J. Showalter

Love Lifted Me

Music by Howard E. Smith

Near the Cross

Music by William Howard Doane

Nearer, My God, to Thee

Music by Lowell Mason

O Come, Angel Band

Music by William Batchelder Bradbury

The Old Rugged Cross

Music by George Bennard

Onward, Christian Soldiers

Music by Arthur S. Sullivan

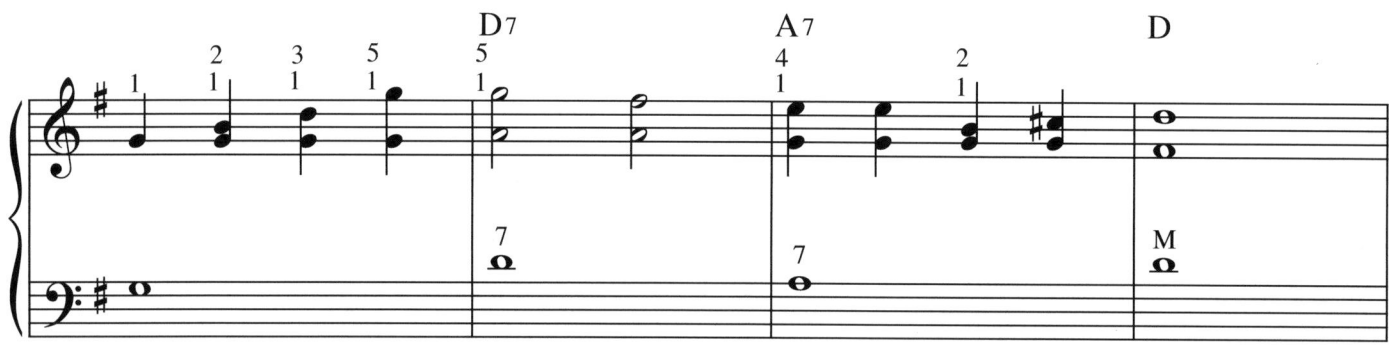

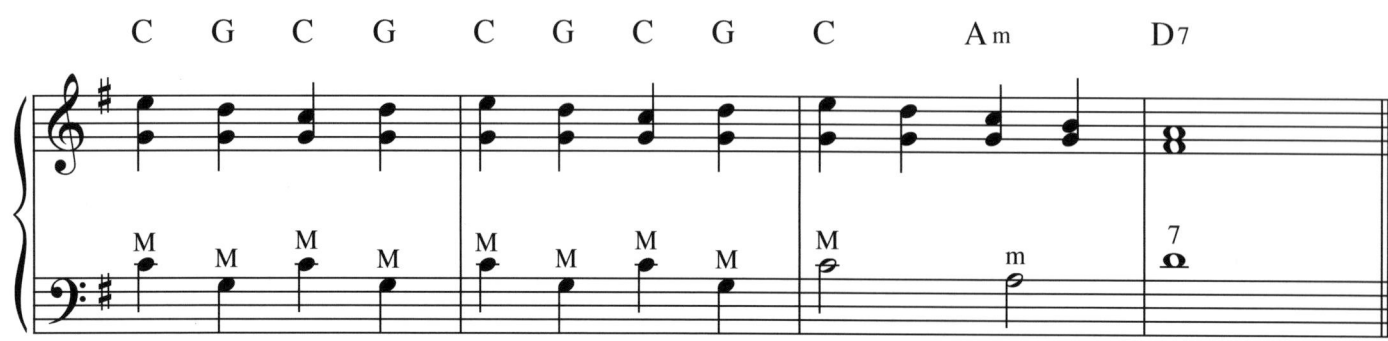

Precious Memories

Music by John Braselton Fillmore Wright

Rock of Ages

Music by Thomas Hastings

Shall We Gather at the River?

Music by Robert Lowry

Softly and Tenderly

Music by Will Lamartine Thompson

Swing Low, Sweet Chariot

African American Spiritual

There is a Fountain

Traditional

The Uncloaded Day

Music by Josiah Kelley Alwood

We'll Understand It Better By and By

Music by Charles A. Tindley

What a Friend We Have in Jesus

Music by Charles Crozat Converse

When the Roll is Called Up Yonder

Music by James Milton Black

When We All Get to Heaven

Music by Emily Divine Wilson

When the Saints Go Marching In

Traditional

Will the Circle Be Unbroken

Music by Charles Hutchinson Gabriel